Animals in Heaven

By Dr. Rexella Van Impe

Adapted from Dr. Jack Van Impe's classic work
Animals in Heaven

ANIMALS IN HEAVEN
© 2021 Jack Van Impe Ministries
Printed in the United States of America
International Standard Book Number:
1-884137-35-0
Cover design by: J. David Ford and Associates,
Frisco, Texas
ALL RIGHTS RESERVED

No part of this publication may be reproduced, stored in a retrieval system, or transmitted, in any form or by any means, electronic, mechanical, photocopying, recording, or otherwise, without the prior written permission of the publisher.

All Scripture quotations are from the King James Version of the Bible.

Jack Van Impe Ministries
P.O. Box 7004
Troy, Michigan 48007-7004
In Canada:
P.O. Box 1717, Postal Station A
Windsor, Ontario N9A 6Y1
www.jvim.com

Table of Contents

Introduction   i

Prologue   iii

God Loves Animals   1

Do Animals Have Feelings? Intellect? Purpose?   5

The Mystery Solved   11

Don't Just Take Our Word For It   15

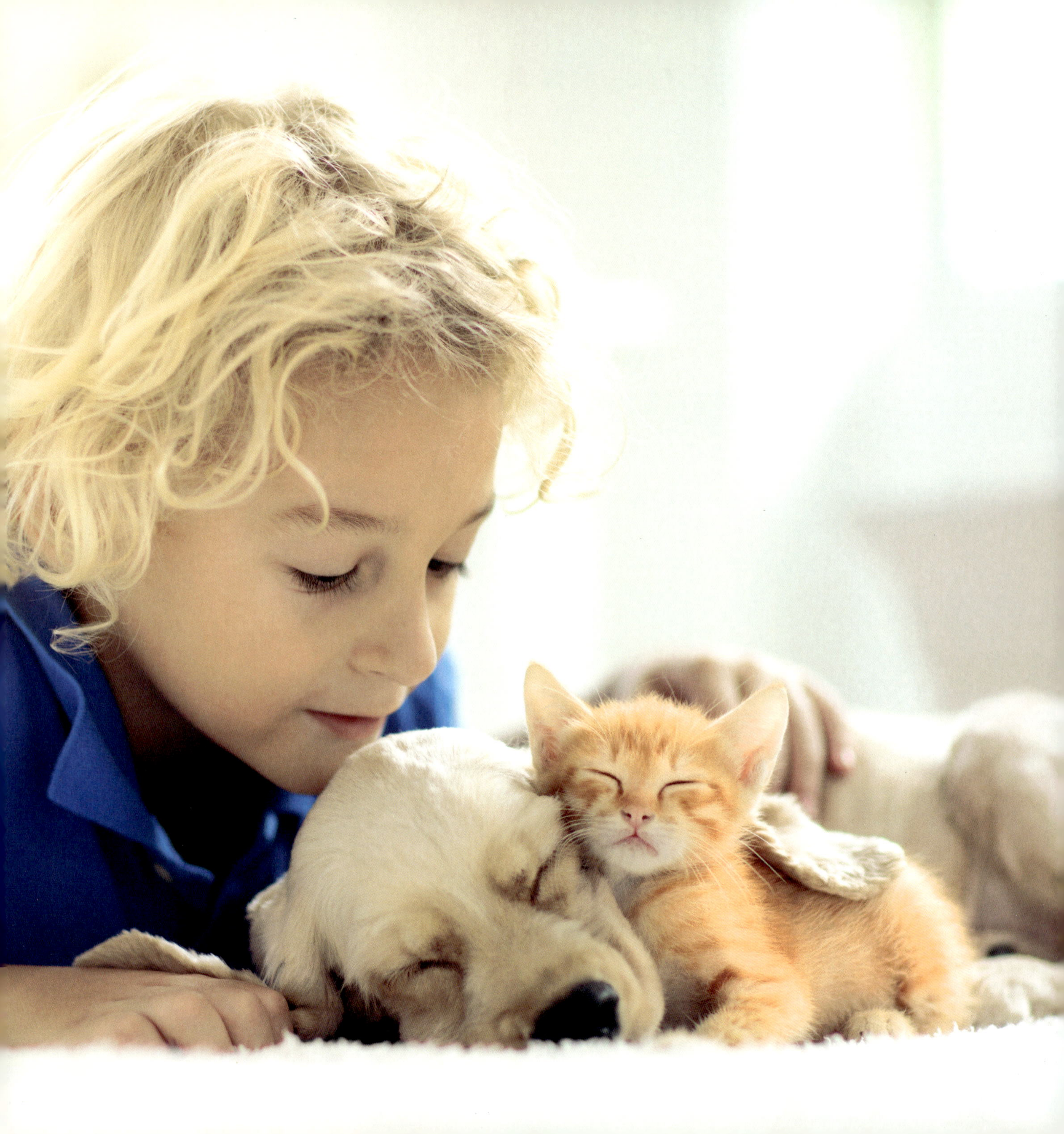

Introduction

Will there be animals in heaven?

In John 14:3, Jesus promises, "I go to prepare a place for you..."

What a beautiful and glorious thought for those of us who love Him!

Our future realtor, land developer, and construction supervisor is none other than Jesus Himself, and He is designing the perfect eternal home for those who have received His gift of salvation. And the value of every lot in heaven? Priceless, "throne-front" property!

Nothing is more significant about heaven than the fact that those who have accepted Christ as Lord and Savior will spend an eternity in His presence, joining the angels to praise His holy name.

And yet, questions about heaven are many! Over the years, Drs. Jack and Rexella Van Impe were asked one specific question again and again: "Will my precious Fido ... or Spot ... or Buttons ... be in heaven?"

Before he went to be with Jesus in 2020, Jack spent many hours researching this very topic with his beloved wife ... and their findings — about animals and their place in this world, and the next — are shared with you here in the following pages.

Be encouraged ... God's Word has good news!

*All verses KJV, unless otherwise noted

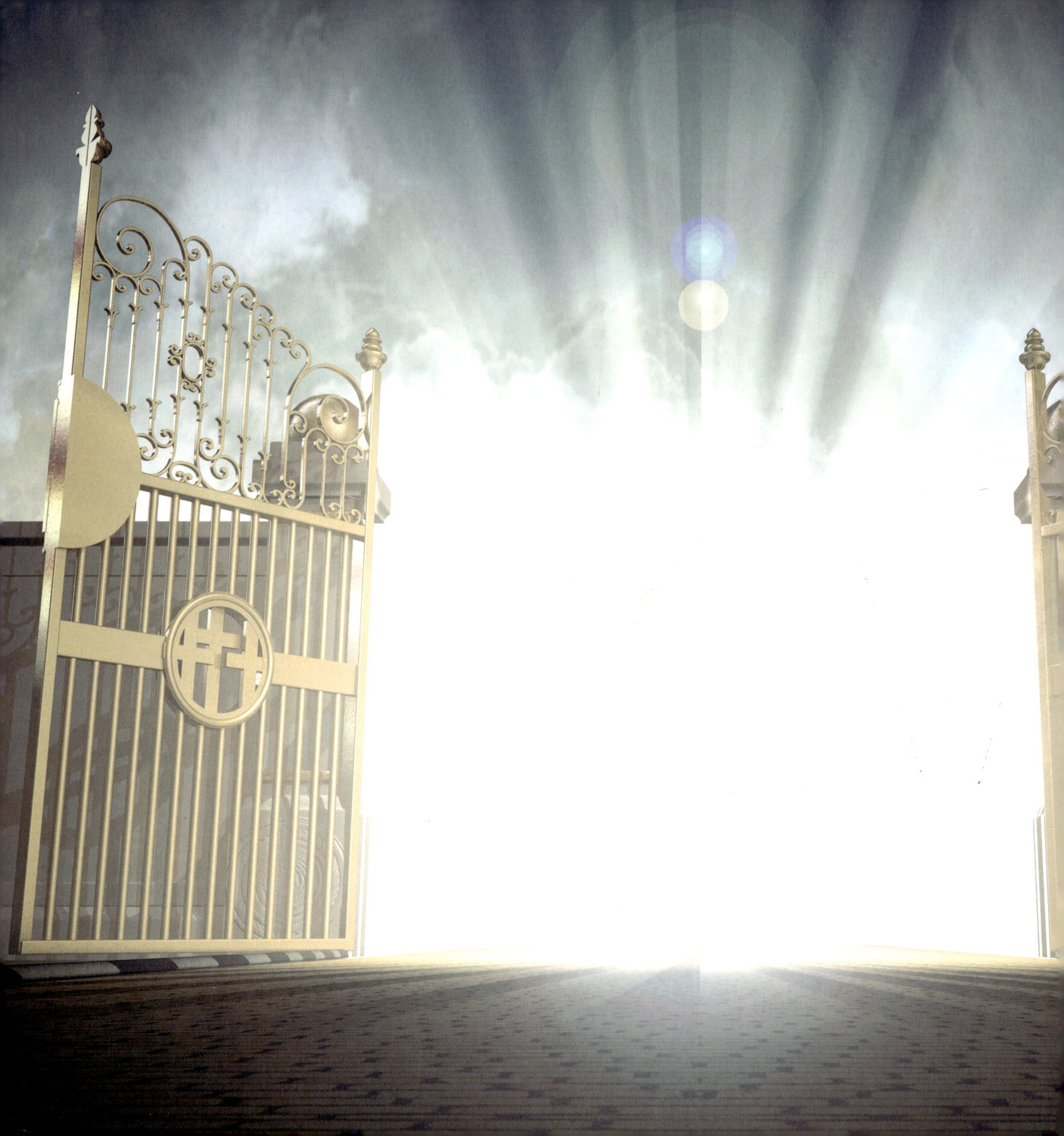

Prologue

To make you smile...

Two mice went to heaven. St. Peter met them at the gate, saying, "Look around for a couple of weeks and come back and tell us how you like it here."

They said, "But we're little mice, St. Peter. Could we have a pair of roller skates to get around faster?"

St. Peter willingly obliged the little ones and sent them on their way.

A week later, Morris the cat came to heaven and, once again, Peter said, "Morris, look around for two weeks, and report after that period of time to tell me how you like it here."

Another week passed. It was time for the mice to report back to Peter, but ... they never arrived.

Then, at the conclusion of his two-week trial period, Morris appeared. St. Peter inquired, "How do you like it here?"

"Oh boy," Morris exclaimed, "I like it!"

"What do you like most about heaven?" was Peter's next question, to which Morris joyfully proclaimed...

"Meals on wheels!"

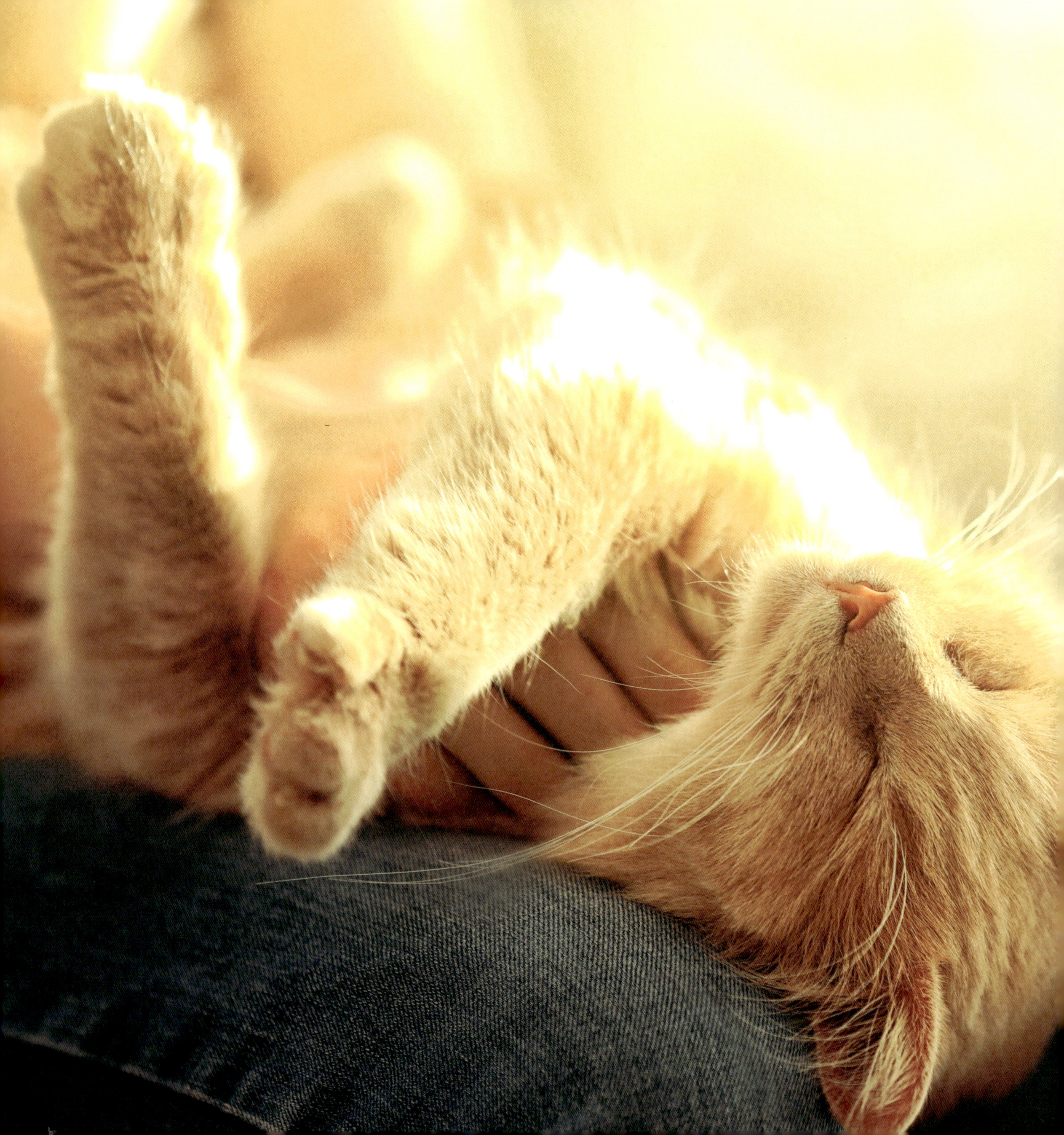

Chapter 1
God Loves Animals

According to a 2019-20 survey by the American Pet Product Manufacturing Association, 67% of U.S. households own a pet. Here is a breakdown:

- Fresh-water fish — 11.5 million households
- Cats — 42.7 million homes
- Dogs — 63.4 million
- Birds — 17.3 million
- Small, caged animals like rabbits or gerbils — 5.4 million
- Reptiles — believe it or not, 4.5 million!

Jack and I had several pets over the years, each one dearly and deeply loved! Our first cat, Fenica, was a stray that joined our family shortly after we married. After she passed away, we picked up Fenica II from the Michigan Humane Society. She's the only one who could interrupt Dr. Jack Van Impe in his study … and get away with it! I always thank the Lord for the beautiful memories I have of our animal children.

We cared for Bon-Bon, too … and the newest member of our family, Angel. Before Fenica II passed away, Jack and I were looking out on our patio while having our morning coffee, and we had quite a surprise. A kitty we'd noticed under the porch next door was now six months old and had four babies of her own. Oh my, you can imagine what we both agreed to do! I brought out a heated cat bed, and she immediately put her four kittens inside. Jack and I agreed we needed to help care for them … and as they began to grow, we decided to try to find homes for them.

The gentleman who helped us with our yard at the time said he would love to take two of them — one for each neighbor, because they loved kittens and the pets would be given a good home. The other two we took to the veterinarian (along with their mother) to get their shots. The vet said, "Oh, can I keep one?" — *of course!* — and the other kitten was taken to a local farm.

We kept the mother, and after watching her we named her Angel. Jack wanted to bring her inside, and even the vet asked us if we were sure about trying to domesticate a feral cat. Well, friend, we brought her inside and she lived up to her name. She and Fenica II got along amazingly well. While Angel is still with me and just had her 16th birthday, I am truly grateful that Jack and I brought her in to be a part of our family. Fenica II has passed on, but Angel enjoys her home, and I enjoy her.

Most everyone loves animals. Think about all the dogs and cats that have been in the White House alone, from George Washington's beloved Greyhound, Cornwallis — to Joe Biden's German Shepherd, Major. Winston Churchill had a poodle named Rufus, and nobody could eat until Rufus, sitting beside him, had his food.

Pets bring a sense of calm and compassion to a home. When it seems no one else loves you, your pet always comes through! Have you ever walked out of the room and returned a few minutes later to find your dog jumping all over you in excitement? As if you'd been gone for days! That's devotion! Unconditional love at its best.

Because humans were created in God's image, we are built to love! The Scriptures are clear: God formed the "birds of the air" and "beasts of the field." He loves His creation, and He requires us to do the same.

Here are some biblical examples …

Of God's care for animals:

- "Are not two sparrows sold for a penny? Yet not one of them will fall to the ground outside your Father's care" (Matthew 10:29 NIV).

- "What man shall there be among you, that shall have one sheep, and if it fall into a pit on the sabbath day, will he not lay hold on it, and lift it out?" (Matthew 12:11).

- "And out of the ground the Lord God formed every beast of the field, and every fowl of the air; and brought them unto Adam to see what he would call them" (Genesis 2:19).

- "Of every clean beast thou shalt take to thee by sevens, the male and his female: and of beasts that are not clean by two, the male and his female" (Genesis 7:2).

Of godly men caring for animals:

- **King Solomon** — "A righteous man regardeth the life of his beast" (Proverbs 12:10).

- **Moses** — "Thou shalt not see thy brother's ass or his ox fall down by the way and hide thyself from them: thou shalt surely help him to lift them up again" (Deuteronomy 22:4).

- **King David** — "Praise the Lord from the earth, ye dragons, and all deeps ... beasts, and all cattle; creeping things, and flying fowl" (Psalm 148:7-10).

- **Isaiah** — Mentions 11 different animals that will be present in the Millennium, as well as the accord that will exist between the wolf and the lamb, the leopard and the young goat, the calf and the lion, etc. (Isaiah 11:6-9).

- **Paul** — In Romans 8:19-21, Paul refers to all of creation waiting in "earnest expectation ... for the manifestation of the sons of God" — that "the creature itself shall be delivered from the bondage of corruption into the glorious liberty of the children of God."

All of creation, including the animals, has experienced the decay and death of our sin-sick world ... but will one day revel in the completion of God's plan of redemption and the perfection of an eternity in heaven.

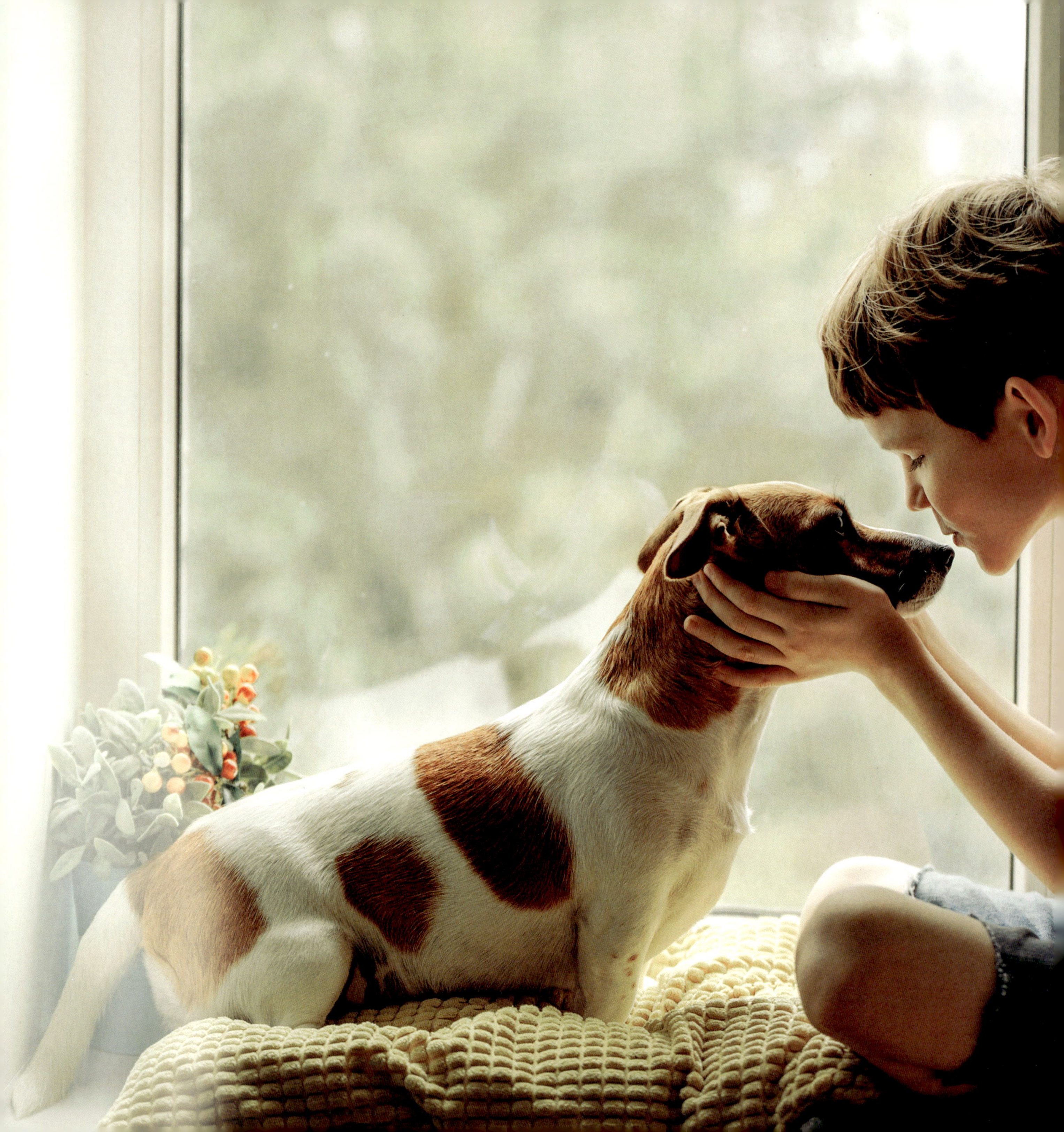

Chapter 2
Do Animals Have Feelings? Intellect? Purpose?

Before we discuss whether animals will be in heaven, let's look a moment at this most magnificent of God's creation. What beauty and creativity our Lord displayed when He filled the seas and skies and earth with living things!

While man was truly His crowning achievement, God didn't skimp on the animals!

Animal Emotions

We've all heard the stories ... animals at the zoo displaying signs of mental illness: an elephant dying of grief after losing a partner; family pets becoming depressed when their owners get divorced; chimpanzees nurturing and loving their babies.

And there was a story in the news some time ago hailing "Scarlet, Cat of the Century." Scarlet went back into a burning building in Brooklyn, NY, five times to pull each of her kittens to safety, even after being burned significantly. She was a mother on a mission to save her family!

But what does the Bible say?

In Luke 16, we read the story of the rich man clothed in purple and fine linen, who "fared sumptuously every day." Meaning, he had plenty of good food to eat! Outside the gate of his home, a beggar "covered in sores" cried out for the crumbs off this man's lavish table. It's an incredible story of God's grace to the beggar — and His contempt for the snobby rich man, who could not be bothered to help someone in desperate need.

One ended up in heaven, carried to glory by the angels. The other?

Relegated to a lifetime of torment and torture in hell.

Here's the part of the story that speaks to the animals: In verse 21, it says the "dogs came and licked his sores." Was this tidbit included just to gross us out? No! We believe the dogs were drawn to show compassion to Lazarus when the rich owner of the house would not. They comforted him — and even provided relief for his suffering.

A Pet's Purpose

Pets do more than just wag a tail with joy when we walk through the door. More than just cuddle up at our side to sleep. More than just bring us comfort and care at our lowest moments. And certainly more than just keeping our floors crumb-free (although we are sure thankful for this!).

Animals have truly displayed the capability to be worthwhile companions...

- Providing eyes for the blind and ears for the deaf.
- Emotionally supporting those suffering with PTSD, anxiety, depression.
- Capable of operating sophisticated machines for the paralyzed.
- Providing friendship and an antidote for loneliness for the elderly.
- In addition, studies have shown that pets often have a therapeutic effect on sick or disturbed children.

You might recall instances when earthquakes, mudslides, or some other natural disaster buried humans alive. Dogs were brought in to run the scene, sniff under rocks, find signs of life. They are also capable of sniffing out illegal drugs, with a sense of smell anywhere from 30,000 to 80,000 times stronger than that of a human.

Do Animals Have Feelings? Intellect? Purpose? | 7

Everything these animals give to us demands that we give back love and devotion to them!

Animal Intelligence

"But ask now the beasts, and they shall teach thee; and the fowls of the air, and they shall tell thee" (Job 12:7).

Did you know...

- The Eurasian Crane flies 2,500 miles from Spain to the Boreal Forest?
- The White Stork flies 3,100 miles from central Africa to western Europe?
- The Bald Eagle flies 1,800 miles from the American West to Alaska?

Birds were created by God with incredible internal navigations systems! They don't need GPS with turn-by-turn directions. They never get lost.

There's no end to the intelligence within the animal world — because God created them that way.

Man's Best Friend

"He is your friend, your partner, your defender, your dog. You are his life, his love, his leader. He will be yours, faithful and true, to the last beat of his heart. You owe it to him to be worthy of such devotion."

—Anonymous

The Monarch Butterfly

God's creativity on full display can be found in the life cycle of the beautiful Monarch Butterfly.

A first-generation butterfly, born in the northern United States or Canada, takes on the first leg of its journey South before winter each year. Two weeks in, it mates and dies. Then, the second-generation takes over. About four generations in, the butterfly has made it to its destination, high atop the mountains of southwestern Mexico. As many as 3,000 miles have been covered.

The final generation Monarch is born there. It is a "super" variety — and after its transformation, it travels the entire distance to its "summer home" up North. It lives, on average, eight months.

A miraculous, beautiful reminder of God's grand design for each and every creature on earth!

In the Bible, we read of two instances where animals took on human qualities, and impacted humanity as a result.

- In the Garden of Eden, the serpent spoke and said to Eve, "Ye shall not surely die" as he persuaded her to eat the forbidden fruit (Genesis 3:4). She ate, and so did Adam. Sin entered the world with their disobedience.

- Then in Numbers 22:1-33, the story of the apostate preacher is found. He backslid — turned from the faith. And what brought him back? A talking donkey! Second Peter 2:16 says, that "the dumb ass speaking with man's voice forbad the madness of the prophet."

To make you smile…

Other animals speak, too. One time, Jack was staying at the home of a friend before preaching at a crusade. During the day, Jack decided to find a quiet room in the house to get alone with God, pray, and seek the Lord.

Out loud, he prayed, "Oh, Lord, show me what I should preach tonight."

He heard a voice saying: "You must be born again."

Jack said, "Lord! Are you talking to me?"

Again and again, the voice repeated, "You must be born again."

Confused and intrigued, he looked around, and there it was … a parrot perched on a stick in the corner of the room! God used that bird to press on his heart that he was to preach John 3:7 at the crusade. Scores of people accepted Christ as Savior!

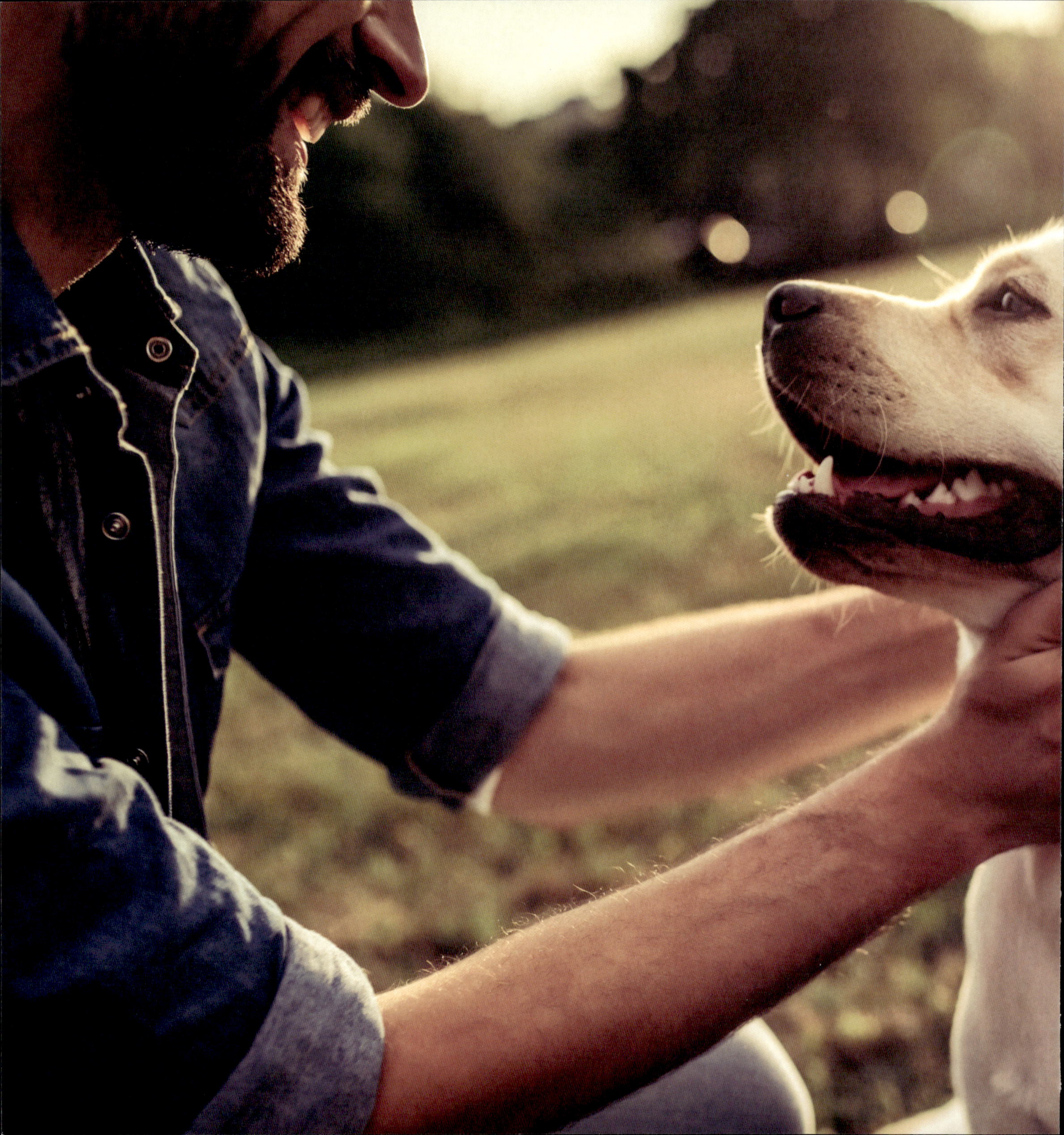

Chapter 3
The Mystery Solved

"And the glory of the Lord shall be revealed, and all flesh shall see it together" (Isaiah 40:5).

So far, we have determined that God made animals special!

They have feelings. They possess intellect. And God has imbued purpose — the ability to do great things for mankind and our world — into the minds of our pets.

But the question remains: Will we see them in heaven?

According to Isaiah 40:5, the answer is yes! When the glory of the Lord is revealed, all flesh will see it together!

Three Proofs

№1 — If you look at 1 Corinthians 15:39, it is established that animals are flesh: "All flesh is not the same flesh: but there is one kind of flesh of men, another flesh of beasts, another of fishes, and another of birds."

Since Isaiah says, "all flesh," we must conclude that, while the flesh of animals is different from ours, they will still be included in the heavenly realms someday.

№2 — Furthermore, we believe that everything on earth is a picture or pattern of things in heaven (Hebrews 9:23). Earth, beginning with the Garden of Eden, is filled with animals, so God's eternal home must certainly contain all types and varieties of His animal creation, too.

And the beautiful thing? Heaven will be much like the Garden of Eden ... with tame, domesticated lions, tigers, and bears! Oh my!

But what about your beloved dog? Or our precious rescued stray cat? The Bible does not specifically state anything concerning our pets being taken upon death or the Second Coming to an eternal home. However, we believe the promise of Psalm 84:11, that "no good thing will he withhold from them that walk uprightly." If we ask of our Lord, our pets will join us in heaven.

Q: Will our pets praise God in heaven?

A: Yes! Read Psalm 148:2-14. Dragons, fish in the sea, beasts, cattle, and all creeping things are admonished to praise the Lord. And Psalm 150:6 says, "Let everything that has breath praise the Lord." It's possible here on earth for animals to praise the Lord, so it will surely happen in heaven!

№3 — Take some time now to read Revelation 5:9-14.

It's a beautiful passage full of praise and adoration for the King. The Rapture has occurred, and the saints are in heaven singing a song around the Throne of Grace.

But there are other voices there — besides the Raptured saints. There are angels ... and beasts (animals) ... and "every creature which is in heaven, and on the earth, and under the earth, and such as are in the sea, and all that are in them, heard I saying, Blessing, and honor, and glory, and power, be unto him that sitteth upon the throne, and unto the Lamb forever and ever."

The animals are there, and they are worshipping God!

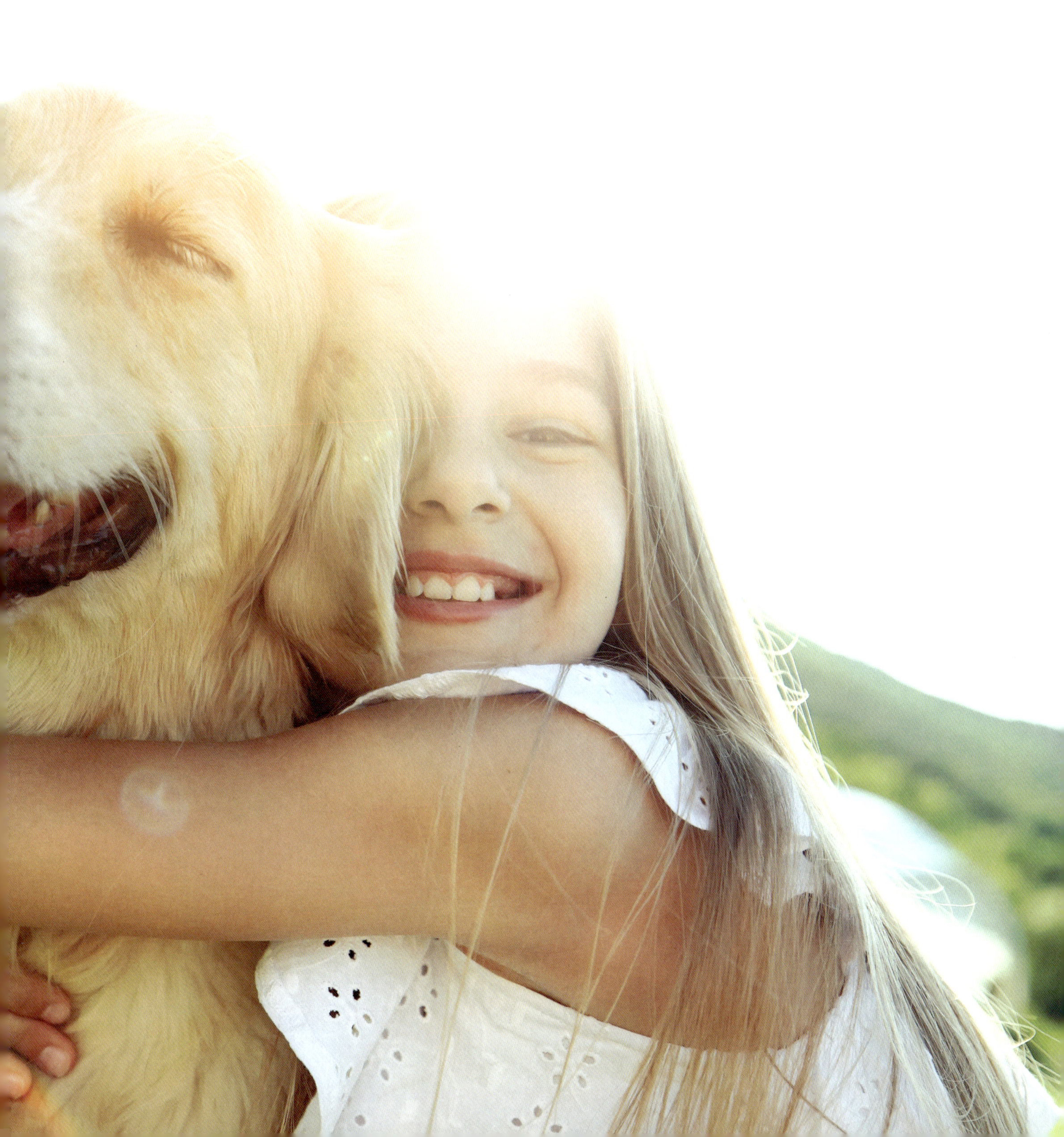

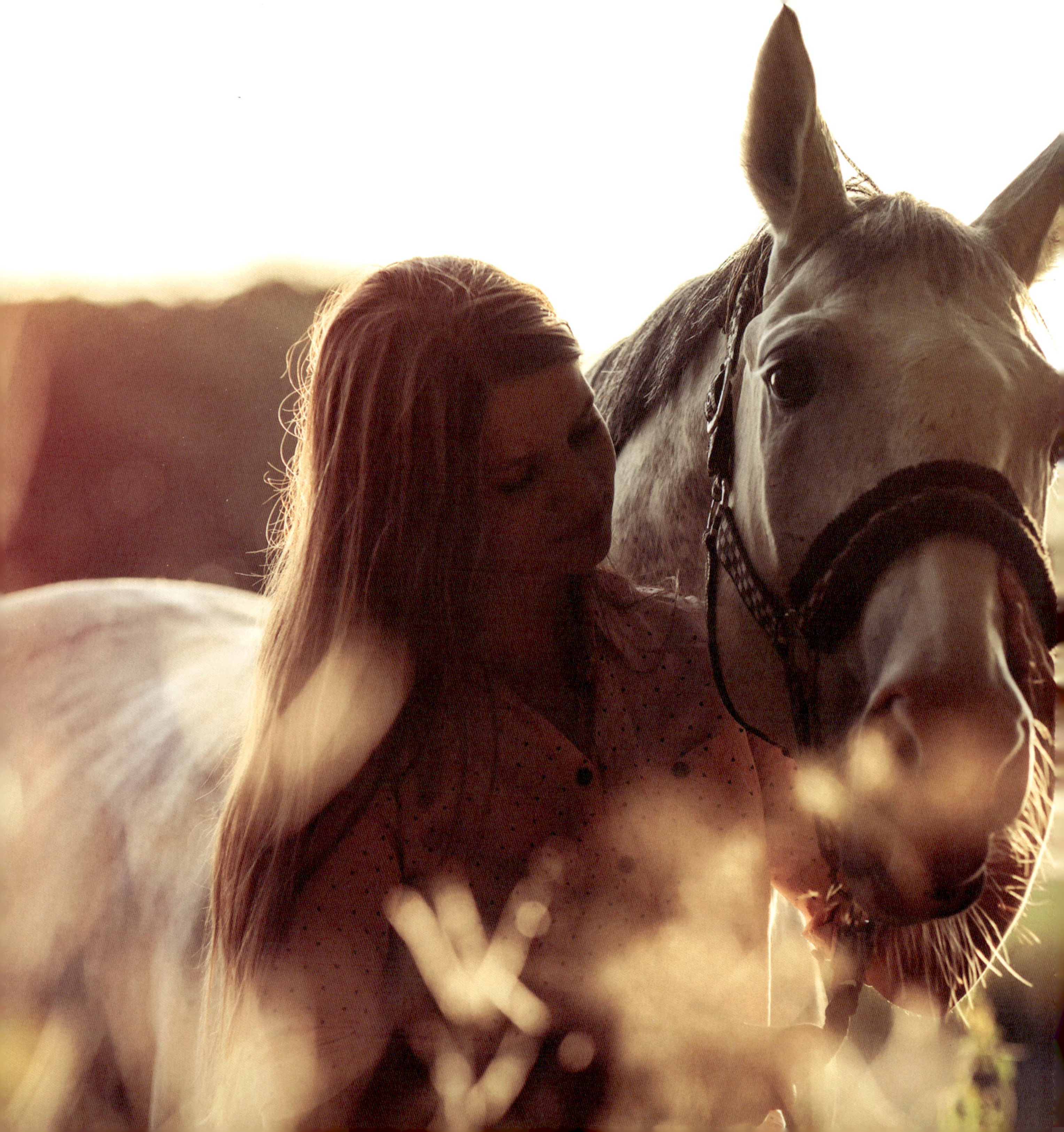

Chapter 4
Don't Just Take Our Word For It…

Some of the greatest minds in Christian history share our belief that animals, specifically pets, will be raised along with the saints at the Rapture. Many of the men we list here were referring to the passage Romans 8:21-23.

> …Because the creature itself also shall be delivered from the bondage of corruption into the glorious liberty of the children of God. For we know that the whole creation groaneth and travaileth in pain together until now. And not only they, but ourselves also, which have the firstfruits of the Spirit, even we ourselves groan within ourselves, waiting for the adoption, to wit, the redemption of our body.

John Calvin. Famous reformer, Bible teacher, and commentator. He said, "Creatures are not content in their present state, and yet they are not so distressed that they pine away without a prospect of a remedy." That prospect? Heaven!

Dr. E.D. Buckner. Author of *The Immortality of Animals*, 1903. He taught the following regarding Romans 8: "Paul helps us to understand that this suffering of animals shall not be hopeless, but that they shall be delivered together with man from the bondage of corruption."

Dr. William R. Newell. American Bible teacher and pastor, Assistant Superintendent of Moody Bible Institute, 1895. He said, "We should be tender and patient toward animals, for they are in a dying state — until our bodies and theirs are redeemed."

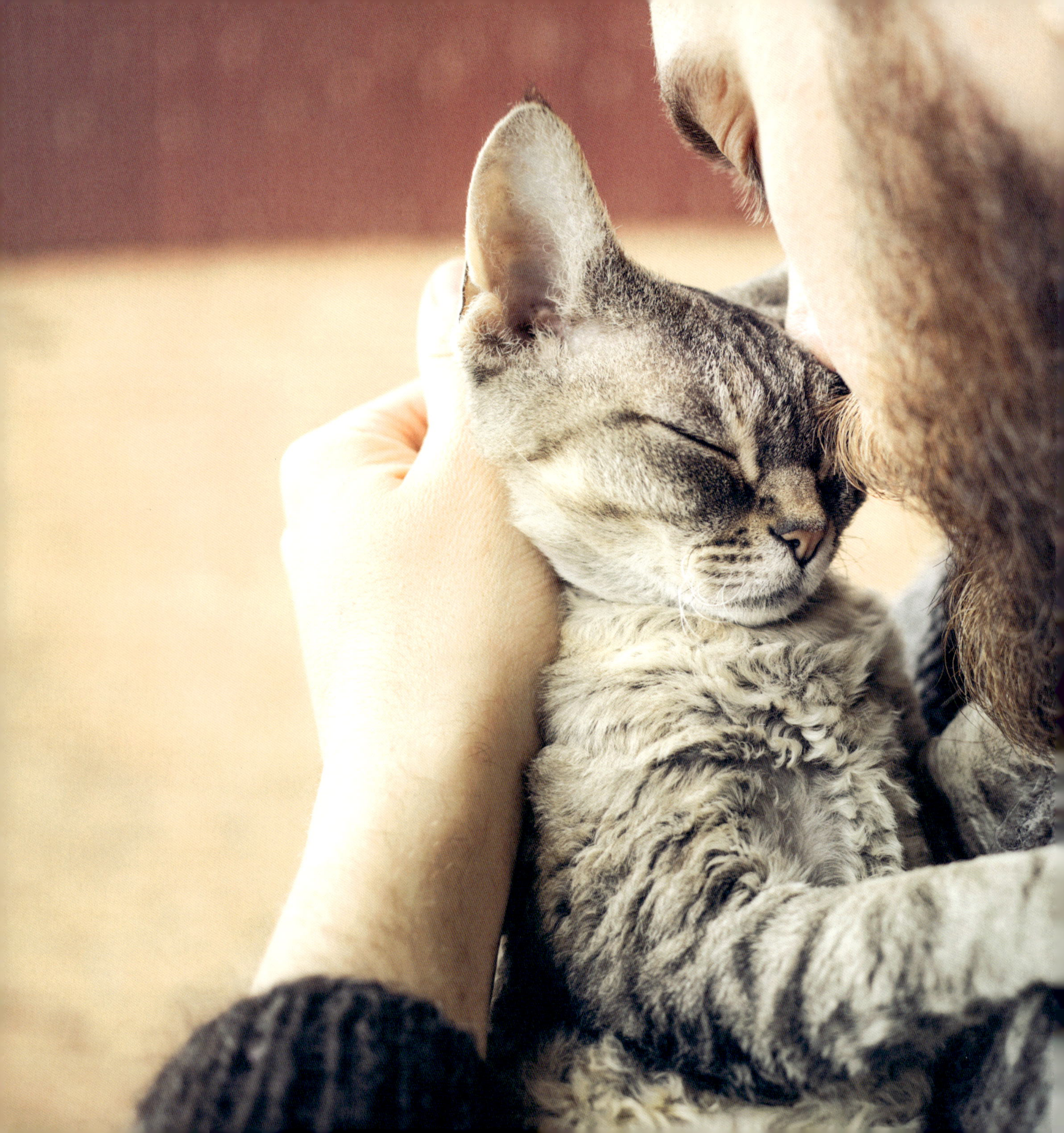

Don't Just Take Our Word For It | 17

Dr. William L. Pettingill. A noted theologian who said, "Animals generally, are now suffering in the bondage of corruption, but in that day their deliverance will come."

Dr. Edward E. Hindson. Evangelist and Bible teacher. "God promises that even all creation will one day be delivered from bondage to liberty."

Dr. John Walvoord. President of Dallas Theological Seminary, 1952-1986. "The creation waits in eager expectation for the Sons of God to be revealed. Then all of nature, inanimate and animate, including animal life, is personified as eagerly waiting for that time when creation itself will be liberated from bondage and decay."

W. A. Criswell. Pastor and Founder, Criswell College. "God has shown a penchant, or fondness, for varieties of life forms, and it would be difficult to imagine that this would not be perpetuated in the heavenlies."

Dr. Billy Graham. World-renowned evangelist. Dr. Graham was asked if animals went to heaven. His response was that God wanted his people happy, and if having their animals in heaven would make them happy, he supposed that was reason to believe they'd be there.

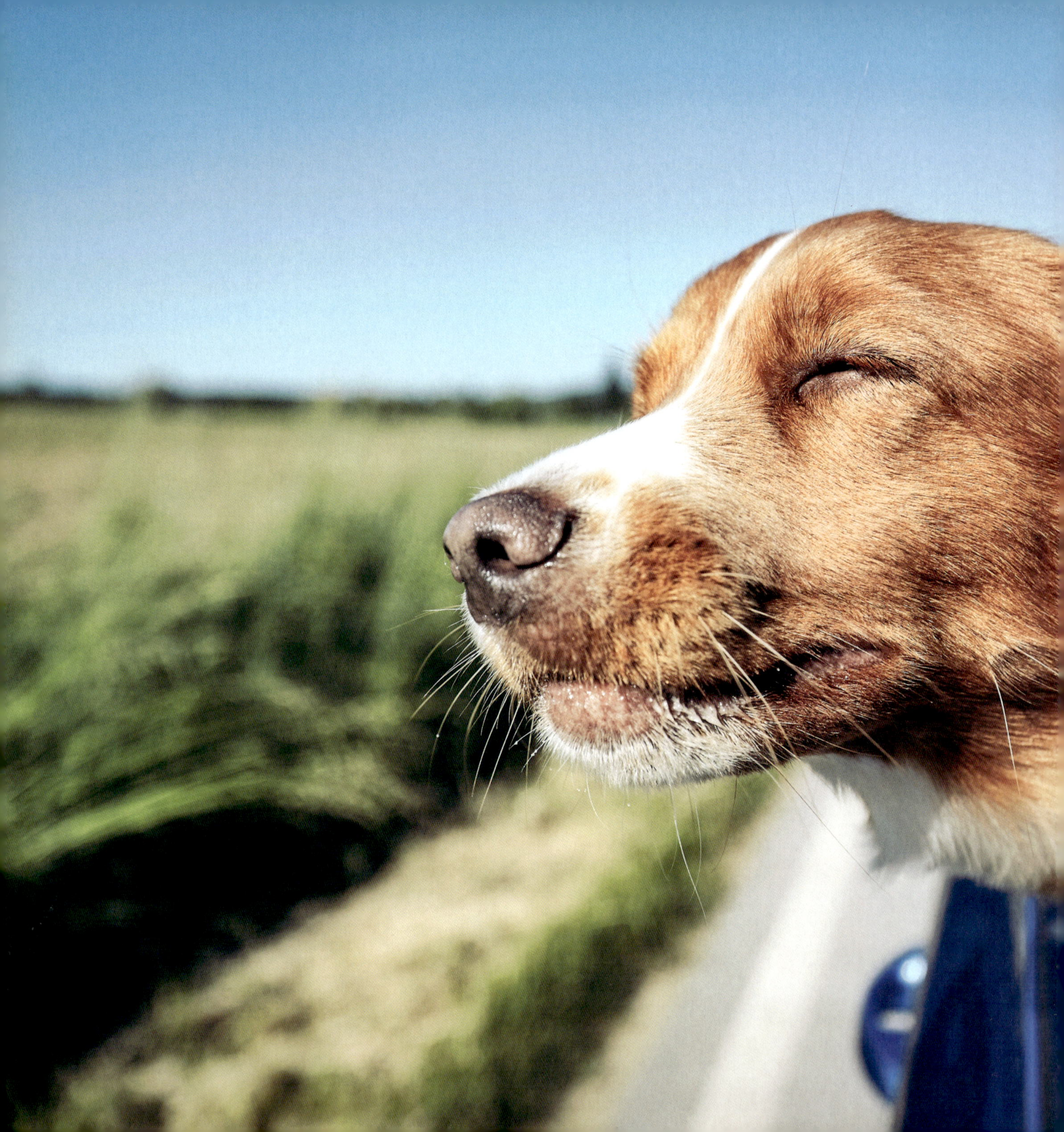

Conclusion

God created man in His image. We are special. Our salvation is His greatest priority.

Nothing is more significant about heaven than the fact that those who have accepted Christ as Lord and Savior will spend an eternity in His presence.

And yet, He loves us so much, He blessed us with "beasts of the field" and "birds of the air," to bring us joy, provide companionship, and even meet our needs. And the message from the greatest theological minds throughout history is strikingly clear: the animals we love will join us in heaven.

It's wonderful to know our animals will be there, praising God alongside us forever!

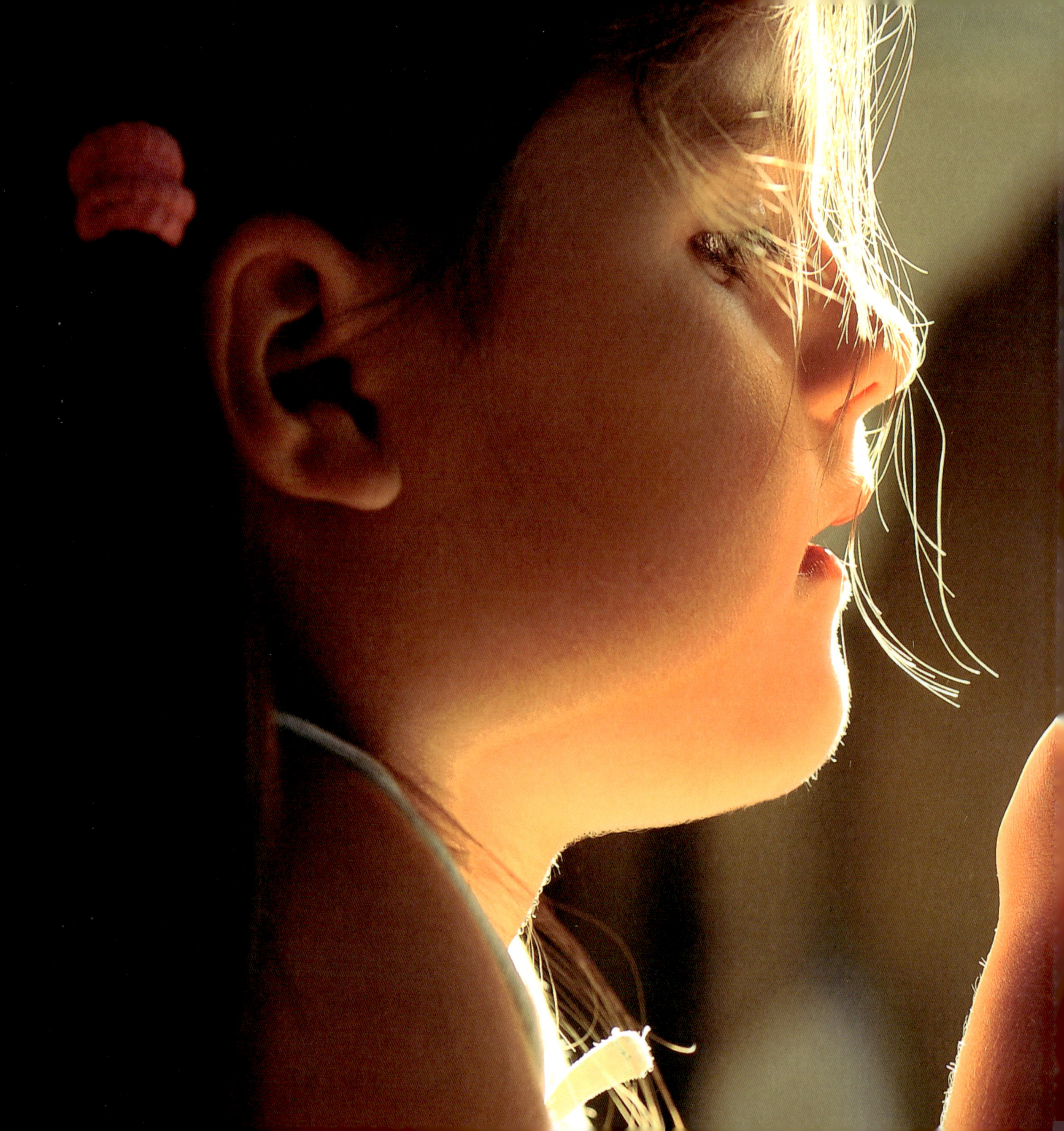

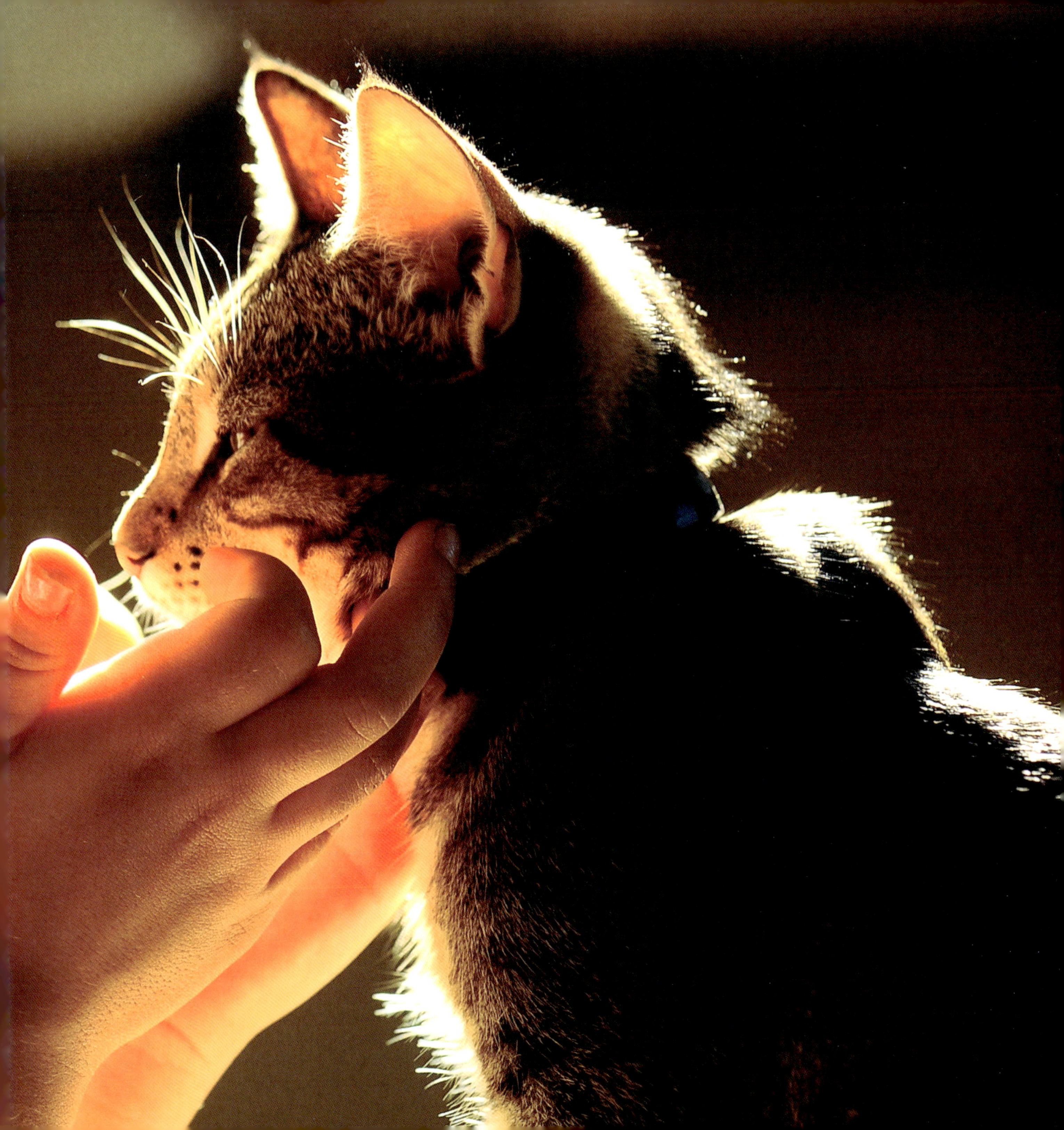

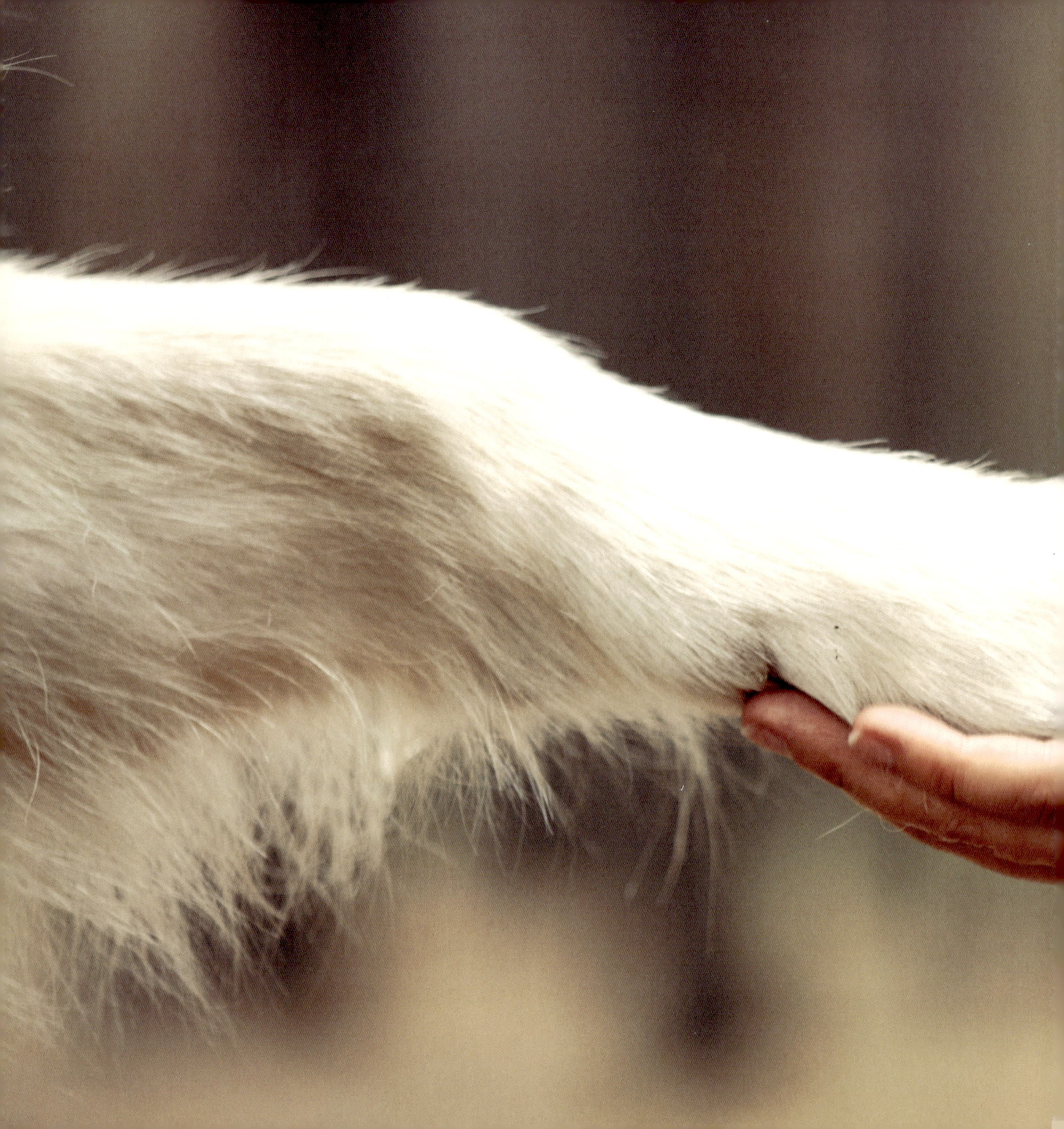

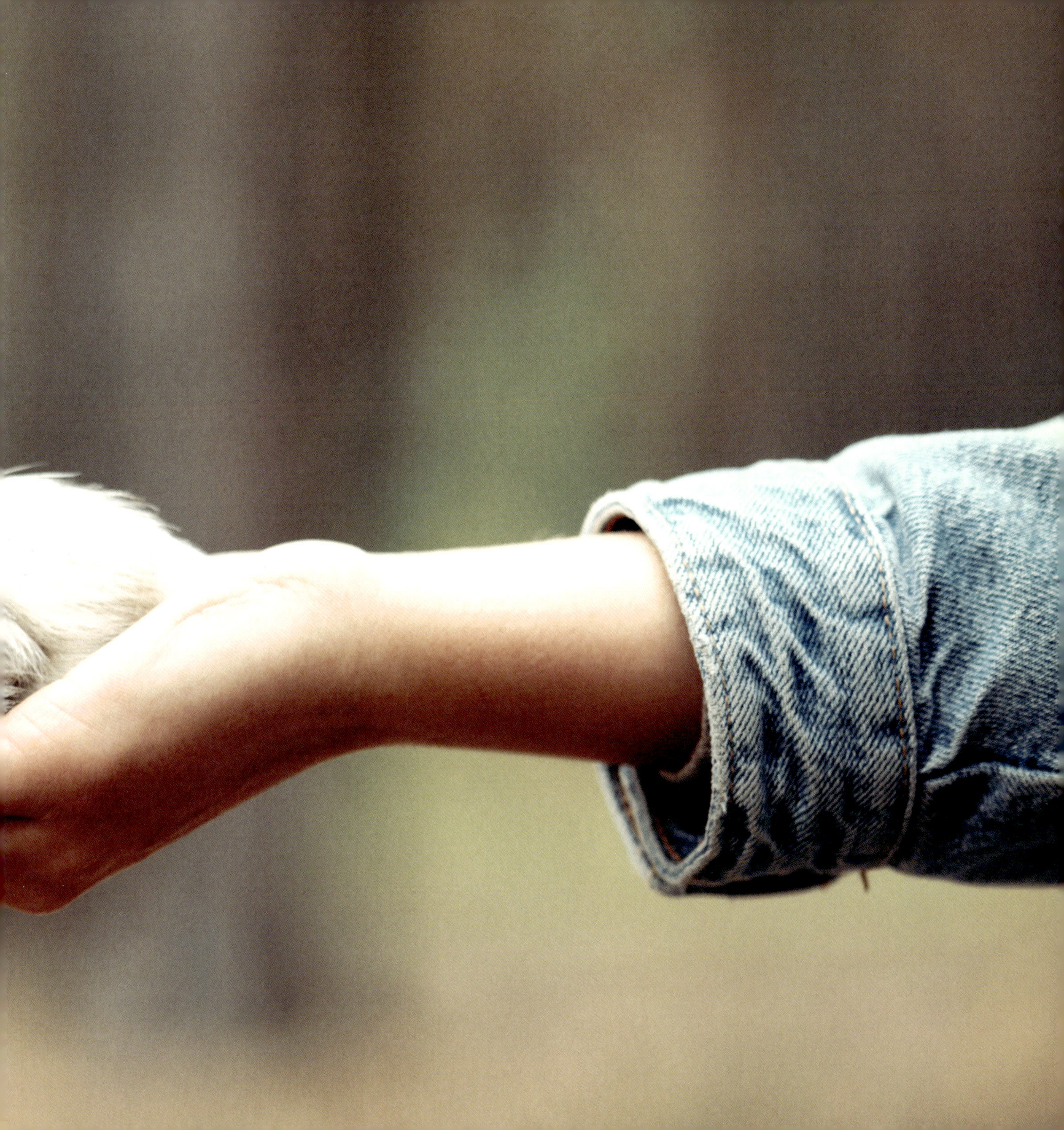

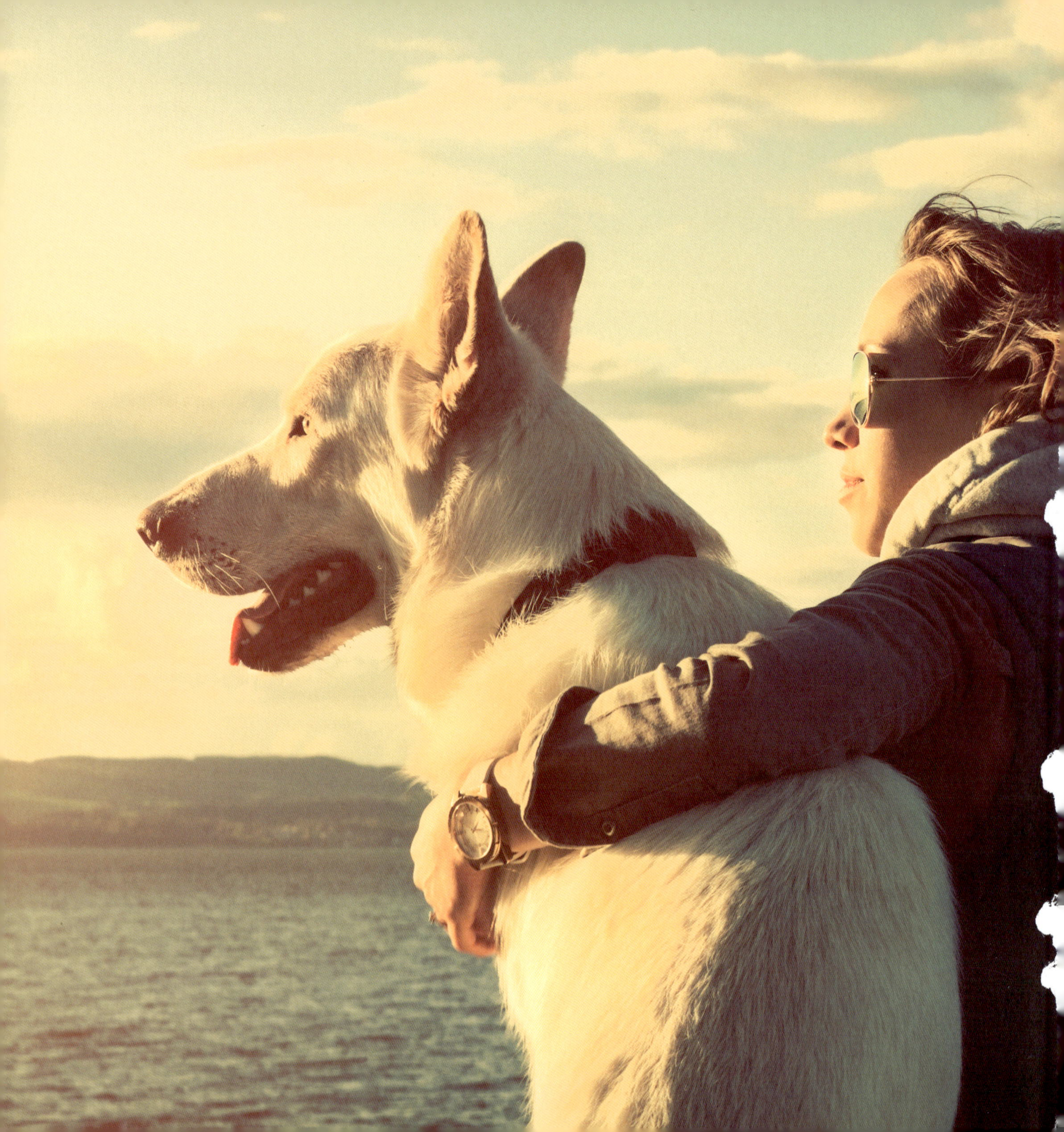